The Drawer Boy

The Drawer Boy

Michael Healey

Playwrights Canada Press
Toronto • Canada

Playwrights Canada Press
The Canadian Drama Publisher
215 Spadina Ave., Suite 230, Toronto, Ontario, Canada M5T 2C7
phone 416.703.0013   fax 416.408.3402
orders@playwrightscanada.com • www.playwrightscanada.com

For production rights, contact Gary Goddard Agency
10 St. Mary Street, Suite 305, Toronto, Ontario M4Y 1P9
phone 416.928.0299 • fax 416.924.9593
goddard@canadafilm.com

The publisher acknowledges the support of the Canadian taxpayers
through the Government of Canada Book Publishing Industry Development Program, the Canada Council for the Arts, the Ontario Arts Council,
and the Ontario Media Development Corporation.

Cover design by Art & Soul. Cover photograph by Howard Chang.
Production editor: JLArt

Library and Archives Canada Cataloguing in Publication
Healey, Michael
The drawer boy / Michael Healey.-- 2nd ed.

A play.
ISBN 978-0-88754-814-7

1. Theatre Passe Muraille. Farm show--Drama. I. Title.

PS8565.E14D73 2005   C812'.54   C2005-902144-6

First edition: May 1999
Second edition: April 2005
Third Printing: August 2008

Printed and bound by Hignell Printing at Winnipeg, Manitoba, Canada

for my parents

The Drawer Boy premiered at Theatre Passe Muraille, Toronto, in February 1999 with the following company:

MORGAN	Jerry Franken
ANGUS	David Fox
MILES	Tom Barnett

Director	Miles Potter
Set Design	Stephan Droege
Lighting Design	Steve Lucas
Costume Design	Michelle Vanderheyden
Sound Design	Jonathan Rooke
Stage Manager	Erica Heyland
Production Manager	Mark Ryder
Technical Director	Jonathan Rooke

—•— **Characters** —•—

MORGAN, in his fifties

ANGUS, also in his fifties

MILES, in his twenties

—•— **Playwright's Notes** —•—

The poem "At The Wedding March" by Gerard Manley Hopkins (1844-89) is quoted in Act Two.

Miles Potter's input at every stage of this play's growth was invaluable. My thanks also to the actors who participated in workshops: Tom Hauff, Gary Rieneke, Raoul Bhaneja, David Fox, Jordan Pettle, Eric Peterson, Jerry Franken, and Tom Barnett. I'm grateful to Ted Johns for his enthusiasm and generosity; to Janet Amos and the Blyth Festival for providing the original impetus; and to Iris Turcott and Brian Quirt for their notes. Thanks to Neil Foster and Factory Theatre, to Kim McCaw and the Banff Playwright's Colony, and to the Toronto and Ontario Arts Councils. Kate Lynch's advice was always helpful and, more importantly, beautifully timed. Plus, she gave me the Hopkins. Thanks as well to Barbara Gordon, Mark Ryder, Allegra Fulton, Steve Lucas, David Kinsman, and Jacoba Knaapen.

Special thanks to Don and Alison Lobb, who fed me dinner and talked about *The Farm Show* like it happened last weekend.

The Drawer Boy

Act One, Scene One

The kitchen of a central Ontario farmhouse, dominated by a large, old oak table; there is a wood stove for heat and a rather modern oven in some ghastly colour. What decorating touches there are, are from the forties. Back door stage left, with a small, unheated mudroom. Downstage a yard (chickens? small vegetable garden?), the barn is offstage right. 1972. Summer.

Lights up. ANGUS alone in the kitchen. Long moment where he sits, eventually gets up, and then starts making sandwiches. Just as he finishes one, MORGAN comes in to the kitchen.

ANGUS   Morgan! Hello!

MORGAN takes the sandwich, eats a couple of bites, and then leaves, taking the sandwich. ANGUS starts to make another sandwich. Meanwhile, MILES wanders into the yard. He looks at the farmhouse, and then leaves. He comes back, and knocks on the door. ANGUS opens the door.

Hello!

MILES   Good morning sir. My name's—

ANGUS   Hey! Who're you?

MILES   …I'm, my name's Miles.

ANGUS   Miles! Hello!

MILES   Hi. I'm from Toronto.

ANGUS   Oh. That's too bad.

MILES	Yes. Uh, I'm here with a group of actors. We're making up a play about farmers.
ANGUS	Oh.
MILES	Yes. I was wondering, could I help out here in any way? We want to spend time with—
ANGUS	We're farmers.
MILES	I… yes. Could you use some help around the farm for the next couple of weeks? Free of charge. I just need a place to stay and the chance to watch you.
ANGUS	Watch me.
MILES	Uh, yes.
ANGUS	Watch me what?
MILES	Well, whatever you do all day. As a farmer.
ANGUS	As a farmer.
MILES	Yes.
ANGUS	I better ask Morgan.
MILES	Okay.
ANGUS	Okay.

ANGUS goes inside. MILES waits. ANGUS heads across the room. He notices the sandwiches and this stops him. He returns to the counter and continues sandwichmaking. As he finishes, MORGAN comes in and takes it.

Morgan! Hello!

MORGAN	Angus. Did I hear you talking?
ANGUS	Talking?
MORGAN	Forget it. Thanks.

MORGAN goes. ANGUS makes a sandwich and starts to eat. MILES waits patiently outside. Slow fadeout of lights, as ANGUS eats and MILES waits.

Act One, Scene Two

> *In the blackout, there is noise off right: a tractor engine being gunned. The following dialogue should be only partially audible over the tractor.*

MORGAN   Alright, now. Alright. Give 'er. Little more… little more.

ANGUS   Give 'er. Give 'er. Give 'er.

MILES   Okay…

MORGAN   You got to line up those parts—

MILES   Right.

MORGAN   —so I can connect them.

ANGUS   Give 'er. Give 'er. Give 'er.

MORGAN   That's it son. That's it. Now back it up into place. Back it up. Reverse. REVERSE!

MILES   Right on, okay. How do I, where's the—

> *The gears grind terribly.*

Oh shit. Where's reverse?

ANGUS   Give 'er. GIVE 'ER! GIVE 'ER!

MILES   Alright. I got it. There we go. Okay!

> *And the motor dies. Pause.*

Wow. Sorry.

ANGUS   Uh oh. Oh shit.

MORGAN   Alright, son. Just—start 'er up again.

> *Sound of the engine starting up again.*

Now. Just back it up slow. That's it. Just a few feet's all. Just a few more…

ANGUS   Give 'er!

MILES   Oooookay. Ooooooookaaaaaay…

Suddenly the engine roars, then dies. After the briefest of pauses, the next occurs all at once.

MORGAN   Jesus Christ! Sonova friggin'—!

MILES   Oh, no. Oh, Jesus.

ANGUS   Jesus Christ! Sonova friggin'! Jesus Christ!

MILES   Are you okay? Sir? Are you—?

MORGAN   Goddam it.

ANGUS   Jesus Christ! Sonova friggin'…

Lights have by now come up. ANGUS runs on, and into the kitchen and as soon as he gets there, he forgets why.

Jesus Christ! Sonova friggin'… Morgan?

MORGAN enters, sits on the stoop, examining his wounded arm. MILES comes in, writing in a small notebook.

MORGAN   Farm's a dangerous place. Put that in yer… play.

MILES   You okay?

MORGAN   Eyuh.

MILES   *(writing)* I'm really, really sorry.

MORGAN   Thought you said you knew how to drive a tractor.

MILES   Just a sec. *(finishes writing)* I really, really thought I did.

ANGUS wanders out to the stoop, and sees MORGAN.

ANGUS   Christ! Morgan! What happened to you?

MORGAN   Angus. You were there. He backed the tractor over me.

ANGUS   Who did?

MORGAN   He did.

ANGUS   *(noticing MILES)* Hello!

MILES   Hi.

ANGUS   Morgan. Who's that?

MORGAN   Angus. Get me a wet towel, willyeh?

ANGUS   Sure.

> *ANGUS goes inside, to the sink. He pauses, and during the following, gets a tablespoon out of a drawer and puts water in it from the tap, carefully walking it out to the stoop.*

MILES   There's no little "R" on your knob.

MORGAN   'Scuse me?

MILES   On your, um… *(He demonstrates gearshift.)*

> Um, I think I should probably not do anything but watch you guys from now on and take notes. If I just do that, rather than actually help you guys around the farm, I think it'd be better for everyone.

MORGAN   If you want to stay here, you'll help out. Don't mind you being here and doing your play-writing, but I can't see having a pair of hands around here that don't do nothing.

MILES   All right. I guess I could, um…

> *ANGUS comes out with the spoonful of water.*

ANGUS   Morgan. Here. *(shoves the spoon in his mouth)*

MORGAN   Thanks. A towel?

ANGUS   You bet.

> *ANGUS goes back indoors.*

MILES   I think I might be better off if I stick to the animals. Animals like me.

MORGAN   Uh huh.

MILES   Could you tell me about the milking operation?

MORGAN   Cows are milked twice a day, milk goes to the dairy. Dairy gives us money.

MILES   Okay, but what's it like? Do the cows mind being milked continually?

MORGAN   Do they mind?

MILES   Yeah, well, you know, how does a cow feel about getting interfered with twice a day?

ANGUS returns with another spoonful of water. Shoves it in.

MORGAN (*to ANGUS*) Thanks. A towel?

ANGUS You bet.

ANGUS goes back inside.

MORGAN How does the cow feel. About getting milked.

MILES Yeah. Do they find it traumatic at all? All the, you know, touching?

MORGAN Well, even though you're from the city, you must know that your cow is the laziest of God's creatures.

MILES Right.

MORGAN And I'm sure you realize that we slaughter some of the cows we got. For eatin'.

MILES Right.

MORGAN 'Bout one a week we slaughter. Keeps the deep freeze full. Maybe you can help with the next one. Well, the way we choose which cow to kill for meat is related to their milk output. Lowest producer gets the axe. The cows know this, and they produce as much milk as they can, to keep from, you know, being chosen.

MILES I see.

MORGAN Otherwise the dang things would stand around all day.

MILES Really.

MORGAN Here's what I suggest you do. Go into the barn, sit down with the cows. At first, they'll seem real casual. But just watch them for a while and before long, you'll see just how much pressure they're labouring under. They're all tense as cats.

MILES Right. Okay! Thanks. (*rises*) Morgan? I'm sorry I hit you with the tractor.

MORGAN Think nothing of it. Hardly a day goes by on most farms when something or somebody doesn't get run over. I expect you'll find that out firsthand.

MILES	Thanks.

MILES exits. ANGUS returns with water, shoves the spoon in MORGAN's mouth.

MORGAN	Thanks. A towel?
ANGUS	Morgan, I'm tired.
MORGAN	Okay.
ANGUS	Morgan? What happened. Did someone get hit? I smell bread.

MORGAN goes to ANGUS and feels his head.

MORGAN	Okay Angus. Get upstairs and get to bed. I'll come up and close the curtains. Go now.
ANGUS	Okay. Sure. The smell… I wonder, I wish… I…
MORGAN	Angus? Upstairs now.

Act One, Scene Three

Later. MORGAN is in the kitchen, making a sandwich. MILES wanders into the yard. He is looking at his notebook, talking softly.

MILES	Mooo. Mooo—Low. Loooow. Lowing. Loooow. Soooooo. Sooooo scared. Don't want to get eaaaten. Muuuust maaaake miiiilk.

MILES practises a bovine look and movements. Satisfied, he makes a final notation and goes into the house.

Morgan. You were right. All those cows are absolutely terrified.

MORGAN	Sandwich?
MILES	Sure. What kind?
MORGAN	Spleen. Beef Spleen.
MILES	Sure. Great. A small one. How's your hand?

MORGAN smacks his limp hand on the counter.

MORGAN   Numb. Some of the nerves are crushed, I expect.

MILES   Oh my God…

MORGAN   Well, at least the throbbing's stopped. If it's not right in a week or so, I'll get it removed.

MILES   You'll…?

MORGAN   Government'll pay for a hook or something. How'er things in the barn?

MILES   Uhh, well, I sat there for a long time, watching your cows. One of them, a brown one—

MORGAN   Which brown one.

MILES   Uh…

MORGAN   Bow-legged brown one or the brown one that smells like a wet sweater?

MILES   The bow-legged one. I guess.

MORGAN   Daisy.

MILES   She kept trying to turn around to look at me. I think she thought I was coming to choose the next one to get, you know. She looked me in the eye, she, Daisy has these eyes that are like brown tennis balls. She stared and stared right at me. For a long time. It felt like we… exchanged something. Daisy's not… next, is she?

MORGAN   *(coming to the table with the sandwiches)* 'Fraid so.

MILES   Jeez. *(eating)* You said this was beef? Tastes like ham.

MORGAN   That's because we feed the pigs to the cows.

MILES   Really?

MORGAN   Well, not the whole pig.

MILES   *(takes out the notebook)* What's it like, being around death and rebirth all the time? To grow things and kill things for a living, year in and year out? You've been here how long?

MORGAN   We bought the place in '42.

MILES   So for 30 years you've been doing this. Planting, nurturing, nourishing, building up; then harvesting, reaping, destroying, eviscerating.

MORGAN   Uh huh.

MILES   Must be… difficult. I mean, you grow wheat and corn out of the dirt, out of literally nothing, then you cut it down and sell it. You raise animals, feed them and house them for years, name them; and then you kill them and eat them.

MORGAN   Uh huh.

MILES   What is that like? How does that make you feel?

MORGAN   Miles, it's an emotional rollercoaster.

MILES   I bet. Is Angus going to have lunch?

MORGAN   Angus is upstairs asleep. He's got one of his headaches.

MILES   Is there something wrong with him?

MORGAN   He gets headaches. Says he sees lights flashing, sometimes he smells bread baking. Lasts for a day, then he's fine. Sometimes, just before a headache comes on, he'll get giddy. Excited. Then I know to put him to bed.

MILES   Was he always like this?

MORGAN   Angus got knocked down by the front door of a house in London in '41 during the bombing. He's got a plate in his skull that keeps the two broken parts of it from rubbing together. Before that, he was just like you or me. We went over together, and came back together. We grew up.

MILES   And you've taken care of him since the war?

MORGAN   He doesn't need much taking care of. Angus's no invalid. I show him how to do things, remind him. He can run the tractor, he can use the stove. Knits. Does the accounts. You should see him with a bunch of figures. Only thing that makes Angus different is he can't remember from one minute to the next. He only knows right now. He won't remember you.

MILES   Ever?

MORGAN	Nope. You'll have to tell him who you are, what you're doing here, probably every morning.
MILES	What do the doctors say?
MORGAN	They say he's normal. For someone who's had done to him what he's had.
MILES	Will he ever, I mean, is he…
MORGAN	Angus's fine. He stays here, does what I've taught him, we're just fine.
MILES	You've lived here alone since the war?
MORGAN	Yup. We bought this land right after. Finish up. Plenty to do this afternoon.
MILES	*(wolfing and rising)* Right. Nothing dangerous I hope.
MORGAN	Nah. Ever gutted anything?
MILES	You mean, what, like cut the guts out of something?
MORGAN	Uh huh. Do you know how to use a chain saw?
MILES	I, uhh. No. No sir, I don't.
MORGAN	Nothing to it. Just remember to hold on tight when things get slippery.
MILES	Think it's a good idea? After the tractor?
MORGAN	Probably not. But they'll be no mollycoddling on this farm while there's work to do. Plus, I'll stand well back.
MILES	They're not going to believe this at rehearsal.
	ANGUS enters, disoriented and in pain. The light hurts him. He's looking for something.
ANGUS	Morgan? Hello. Someone got hit by the… car? Right?
MORGAN	You need to be lying down. You know, Angus.
ANGUS	Right. *(He sees MILES.)* Who're you?
MILES	My name's Miles. I'm staying here with you while I put on a play about farmers.
ANGUS	Tall. You look like, standing there, beside the…. The girl. *(to MORGAN)* Right?

MORGAN   *(to MILES)* You go ahead, meet you in the barn.

MILES   Sure.

> *MILES exits.*

ANGUS   Right?

MORGAN   Angus. Your head hurt?

ANGUS   Well, yeah.

MORGAN   Let's go up, then.

ANGUS   Uh huh.

Act One, Scene Four

> *ANGUS walks into the kitchen, looking for something. He begins his search by staring at an empty space on a wall. Maybe he traces the inverted V of a rooftop with his finger. Eventually, he starts to look around, opening cupboard doors and looking under things. He's on his hands and knees when MILES limps into the farm house, his hands and thighs bleeding. MILES has some trouble getting the door open.*

MILES   Wow. Ow Jeez.

ANGUS   Hullo. Hey. Get outta here.

MILES   Hello, Angus. My name is Miles and I'm staying with you and Morgan to learn about farming so I can write a play about it.

ANGUS   *(throws a hand up in the air)* Hello, Miles. Okay.

> *MILES limps to the sink, starts to tend to his wounds.*

You hungry? Fella?

MILES   I was just out helping Morgan with the hay bales. I musta hauled six hundred of the damn things off the wagon and on to the… escalator thing…

ANGUS	The what?
MILES	The, you know, the thing that takes the bales up to the top of the barn.
ANGUS	Oh yeah, that thing's called the… uh.

ANGUS goes to the sink during the following, gets MILES a spoonful of water.

MILES	The only way to do that's to drag them off the wagon and sorta throw the bale onto the escalator using your leg. Look at my leg.
ANGUS	That's something, alright.
MILES	Morgan looks at me and says: "Folks wear long pants around a farm." I bet this is infected.

ANGUS shoves the water in MILES' mouth.

Thanks.

ANGUS	Uh huh. Help yourself.
MILES	Then I go up into the barn to stack the bales and that's even worse cause there's no air up there, lots of dust but no air, and I have to pick the damn things up, lift them over my head, and pile them up.
ANGUS	You want a sandwich?
MILES	I've done hard things, Angus. I was a hedgehog in a show last year about a group of dead animals. That show was three hours long. *I didn't move.* I've done hard things. And I wasn't about to quit, not with Morgan watching. I just picked them up, one by one, hauled them over to the side of the barn, built a wall of hay. Look at my hands. Splinters inside of exploded blisters.
ANGUS	Yup. That's something, alright.
MILES	"The twine, city boy, pick them up by the twine!" For God's sake. I'm not supposed to be doing this. I'm supposed to be writing a play.
ANGUS	Was it hay or straw you were loadin'?
MILES	I dunno. What's the difference?

ANGUS	Between hay and straw?
MILES	Yeah.
ANGUS	One you eat, and one you sleep in. What are ya, stupid?
MILES	Okay.
ANGUS	I forget which, though.
MILES	Do you think that Morgan's still upset with me over the thing with the tractor?
ANGUS	Thing with the…?
MILES	Running him over with the tractor. I ran him down two mornings ago, remember?
ANGUS	Uuuhhhh. Nope. Tractor, eh?
MILES	Yes. Never mind.
ANGUS	Someone got hit by the tractor?
MILES	Yes, it's okay, Angus. Forget it.
ANGUS	You bet.
MILES	*(points at the fridge)* Angus, what's that called?
ANGUS	That's the, uuuhhh. Nope.
MILES	Is that the refrigerator?
ANGUS	Sure it is.
MILES	Or the stove?
ANGUS	Morgan. We better ask Morgan that.
MILES	It's okay. *(raps on the tabletop)* That's the chair, right?
ANGUS	Chair.
MILES	Angus. What's my name?
ANGUS	Don't you know?
MILES	Do you?
ANGUS	Ha ha.
MILES	Okay.

ANGUS	Okay then.
MILES	My name's Miles.
ANGUS	Hello, Miles, okay.
MILES	Angus? Twelve, fifty-six, one oh seven, twelve again and six seventy-nine.
ANGUS	Uh huh.
MILES	What's my name?
ANGUS	…Oh. Uuuuhhh. Ha ha.
MILES	Okay. Angus. What about those numbers I said. Can you add them up?
ANGUS	Eight hundred sixty-six.
MILES	Right! I think that's right…
ANGUS	Oh, yes.
MILES	How old are you?
ANGUS	Bout your age.
MILES	Oh yeah? Is Morgan our age, too?
ANGUS	Naw. He's an old feller.
MILES	Did you ever fight in the war?
ANGUS	Yes I did. Sure. Princess Pat's. Went to France, went to England. With Morgan.
MILES	What did you have for breakfast this morning?
ANGUS	Ha ha. Sure.
MILES	And what's my name?

ANGUS looks at MILES. He's starting to get worked up.

My name's Miles. Angus. Tell me about your head.

ANGUS	Hurts… sometimes… always…
MILES	How'd you hurt it? Do you know?
ANGUS	Morgan says… they were waiting for… hey. What's your name?

MILES	You tell me.
ANGUS	Don't know. Didn't tell me.
MILES	Angus—
ANGUS	Me too! My name's Angus too! Ha ha ha!
MILES	No, Angus. Listen. Your head. In London, did you get hit by a—
ANGUS	Noo, no. No.
MILES	—in the bombing. By a, a front door.
ANGUS	Front...? No no no no. I did not.
MILES	Is that what happened, or do you just not remember? Morgan said.
ANGUS	Morgan knows. He knows. He tells me. I... the drawer boy. The tall girls.

MORGAN enters.

Hey! Morgan! Hello. How did I get hurt? Was it a front door? Was it?

MORGAN	What? *(to MILES)* What's going on here?
ANGUS	He said. He says you said... uh, he—
MORGAN	Hush now.
ANGUS	No, you said.... Was it the front door? Was it?

ANGUS rubs his eyes and holds his head.

MORGAN	Hush.
ANGUS	No! He said.... The tall girls, did they...?
MORGAN	*(suddenly)* Angus! Make me a sandwich.
ANGUS	Eyuh.

ANGUS gets up and goes to the fridge, he gets out sandwich materials. He is almost instantaneously distracted by this task.

MORGAN	The hell have you been doing?

MILES I didn't mean to upset him. I asked him a few questions about the war. His accident…

MORGAN I thought you were here to find out about farming.

MILES Yes, I…

MORGAN You don't know what you're doing, asking him about that. I told you his memory's faulty. You upset him, he spends the day in bed and I have to do everything by myself. You got questions, ask me. I said I'd tell you everything you need to know *about farming*. Stick to the cows and the chickens. If you can't do that, you'd better leave. Can you do that?

MILES Yes.

MORGAN Miles? You better.

MILES Yes sir. I'm sorry. *(to ANGUS)* Angus? I'm sorry. I'm sorry about what just happened.

ANGUS Okay. Me too. What just happened?

MILES Well, I asked about your—

MORGAN Oh, for God's sake! Nothing!

MILES Sorry, sorry.

Act One, Scene Five

Night. MILES and MORGAN are seated at the table. Dinner is over. ANGUS has finished washing up and starts to make bread. He gets out the ingredients and makes dough throughout the scene. MILES makes notes furiously through the following.

MORGAN *(to MILES)* You know what a steak costs? Per pound?

ANGUS Dollar forty-seven.

MILES Dollar forty-seven?

MORGAN	One dollar forty-seven cents. People scream over a price like that. Drop down dead in the meat aisle when they see that price, but let me tell you something: if the price of that steak had increased in the last ten years as much as the price of a postage stamp, that steak would be a dollar fifty-seven per pound.
ANGUS	Eight point oh-two percent.
MORGAN	If that steak had gone up like the price of a newspaper, it'd cost a dollar seventy-five.
ANGUS	Ten point three percent.
MILES	Per pound.
MORGAN	Per pound. If that pound of steak had gone up like wages have in the last ten years, it'd cost two-oh-eight a pound—
ANGUS	Thirty-nine percent.
MORGAN	—and if it'd gone up like the income tax has, that steak would be three-eighty a pound.
ANGUS	Fifty-eight point three three three three three. Percent.
MORGAN	And wouldn't that make people scream blue murder in the grocery store. We get nothing for what we do. An egg costs nine cents in the store, there's practically an armed uprising in the city over how expensive an egg is. Know how much it costs me to produce that egg? nine point one three cents. Care to guess what my profit margin is on that egg?
ANGUS	Negative eighteen point seven-two cents per gross of eggs.
MORGAN	And if I drop one or two, it gets even worse.
MILES	How can you afford to run a losing business year in, year out?
MORGAN	I make a little on the milk, and that almost evens things out with the eggs. The rest of the debt I put over to next year, until the year when my crops finally go for what they're actually worth. That year, of course, will never come. Public complains about us, they believe all we farmers are making a killing; politicians complain about us, tired of giving us subsidies that just get us to next year, maybe. Kids are

leaving the farms, moving to Toronto; nobody wants to do this anymore! Soon nobody will!

ANGUS Morgan? Why're you shouting?

MORGAN Farms in a strip from Windsor to Montreal provide forty percent of the food for the country and soon they'll all just stop. You'll get your food imported from God knows where, then see how much a pound of steak goes for. You go to university?

MILES Yeah.

MORGAN What'd you study?

MILES English and drama. And political science and geology and law and French. Phys Ed and a little Latin.

MORGAN Uh huh. Graduate?

MILES Well, I was living at this place called Rochdale College, and we really didn't believe that the point was to graduate, we thought that we should be able to—

MORGAN How big a student loan debt didja run up?

MILES That's a little personal, Morgan, I—

MORGAN More than two thousand dollars?

MILES Oh yeah.

MORGAN More than three?

MILES It wound up being around thirty-six hundred dollars. All together.

MORGAN The government gave you more than I paid myself for the last four years.

ANGUS 1968: eight sixty-one; 1969: nine hundred and five; 1970: seven hundred seventy-four, and 1971: seven hundred and ninety.

MORGAN Don't you write that down. I make about the same as everyone else out here, but nobody needs to hear the exact figures from your stage.

MILES Can I use the figures about the pound of steak?

MORGAN   Wish you would.

MILES   This is going to blow people's minds in rehearsal. You know, we all just go to the store, buy some fruit or a steak and never think about where it comes from. Did you ever think of starting up a communal farm?

MORGAN   Eh?

MILES   Have you ever studied the Soviet model? They've been farming communally for decades in Russia and the results are incredible.

ANGUS   Goddamn communists.

MILES   Productivity is up, the people all have enough to eat, money's not a—

ANGUS   *Goddamn communists.*

MILES   —worry. Anybody who looks at it sees it's the wave of the future. Who are your neighbours to the north?

MORGAN   Lobbs. Don and Alison Lobb.

MILES   What if the fence came down between your two places. What if you and the Lobbs agreed—

ANGUS   *Goddamn communists.*

MILES   —agreed that from now on, you'd both work the fields, take turns, maybe even sell one of the tractors, you'd only need the one, one barn for all the animals, an equal division of labour, materials, and profits—

ANGUS   GOD. DAMN. COMMUNISTS!

MORGAN   Angus! Why're *you* shouting?

ANGUS   Was I?

MORGAN   How's that bread coming?

ANGUS puts the bread in the oven.

ANGUS   Done!

Through the following, ANGUS goes outside and stands in the yard. He stares up at the stars and becomes transfixed.

MORGAN   Good. Miles. Let me ask you a question. Now, your answer
          to this question may have a direct bearing on where you
          sleep tonight, on how comfortable a place it is you're
          sleeping in. A place where the humans normally sleep, or
          a place where furred and feathered animals generally lay
          their heads. A place that smells a bit. Miles? How would you
          describe yourself, politically?

MILES   *(after a pause)* Oh. Well, I'm an actor. We don't have
          politics.

MORGAN   I think that's best.

          He goes to the screen door.

          Angus. Don't you let that bread burn.

ANGUS   Bread?

MORGAN   He's ruined more bread.... Where will you be putting on
          this play of yours?

MILES   Ray Bird is lending us his barn for the first show.
          Eventually, we hope to do it all over the county. Hope you'll
          come and see it, both of you. In fact, we're inviting some
          people to a rehearsal day after tomorrow, just so they can
          tell us if we're on the right track. Maybe you'd come to that?

MORGAN   Prob'ly will, seeing as how you're going to give your
          rendition of our cow Daisy.

MILES   Well, maybe not. I did the monologue for the others in the
          show, you know, "Have to make milk, don't want to get
          eaten," and nobody believed it. I couldn't convince anybody
          that cows are petrified all the time. They want to do the
          stereotypical cow, you know, placid, dumb, cud-chewing.
          Bourgeois theatrical cow; that cow that we've seen onstage
          for years and years. And which of course I now know is
          a lie. I said if you want to do a scene about a cow that's a lie,
          we could have stayed in Toronto and made it up out of our
          heads. I said I wasn't going to insult Daisy by portraying
          her without exploring her pain, her anxiety. Her reality. The
          director said okay, fair enough. And then he cut the scene.

MORGAN   Tough break.

MILES   Yeah. So far they aren't using anything I've brought to rehearsal. Remember the day we piled up all those hay bales? I made up a dance, the dance of the hay bale stacker. It got cut, too.

MORGAN   Lemme ask you something.

        He goes to the door.

        Lie down, Angus.

ANGUS   Morgan. Hello.

MORGAN   Lie down if you want to look at them stars. You'll hurt your neck again.

ANGUS   You bet.

MORGAN   *(to MILES)* What happens if none of the… things you make up get put in the show?

MILES   Jeez. I don't know. I guess they'd probably have to kick me out of the collective.

MORGAN   So if you don't produce, you die, is that it?

MILES   …I guess so.

MORGAN   Well, there you go. You have something in common with my cows there.

MILES   You're right.

MORGAN   You got that in common with me, too. I don't produce, I go as sure as you or the cows do.

MILES   Right on. That's good. Mind if I use that?

MORGAN   Guess not.

MILES   Thanks. Think I'll take this upstairs and try to put it into some kind of shape for rehearsal tomorrow.

MORGAN   Right. You'd better get some sleep. We're rotating the crops tomorrow.

MILES   Is that right? That a big job?

MORGAN   Uh huh. We have to dig up all the hay growing on the east side of the field, the hay that gets all the morning sun, and move it to the west side, to get the afternoon sun. Big job. And we have to do it in the dark. Set your alarm for three.

MILES   Three? A.M.??

MORGAN   That's right. And I don't want to have to call you.

MILES   I'll be ready.

MORGAN   See that you are.

MILES   Yes, sir.

> *MILES exits. MORGAN goes outside, and sits on the back step. Silence as he looks at the sky, and at ANGUS.*

MORGAN   Bread in the oven.

ANGUS   Uh huh.

MORGAN   Don't forget.

ANGUS   Aww.

MORGAN   How many?

ANGUS   19,444. Total.

MORGAN   That's a lot.

> *Silence. MILES comes into the kitchen to retrieve his pen. He overhears the following.*

ANGUS   Tell it.

MORGAN   Naw…. Not tonight, Angus.

ANGUS   Sure, tonight. You never tell it.

MORGAN   I tell it daily, you just don't…. Alright. Just… listen.
A couple of boys played shinney and went to school and grew up. One drew pictures of a cabin, fine pictures of the inside and the outside until finally they built the cabin together. Stole nails, played hookey until it was done.

They finished school. One just barely. The other finished easily, but never got his diploma because he wouldn't give back the poetry book.

That one almost went off to school, to keep drawing. The other one never would of. He was all set to work for his father, to start in on the farm. And then they both got called up, both went off to Europe. No school for the one, no farm for the other. They managed to stick together.

They fired their guns straight up in the air and yelled to each other the louder things got. When it got so loud they couldn't hear, they sang. They had three boots between them.

In England they met two girls, one tall and one taller. The taller one liked the drawer, the tall one, the farmer. They talked, they made plans. The girls talked together, the boys talked together.

The tall girl and the farmer would talk all night.

The taller girl and the drawer would walk and talk all night.

One girl would talk to the other boy about the boy she liked, so would the other girl to the other boy about the first boy.

Also they talked in threes.

Drawer boy, two tall girls; farmer boy, two tall girls; tall girl and two boys; taller girl and two boys. They talked to themselves, too.

The plans they made were like something the one boy would draw: Inside and out, all the details mixed and when they were done talking, all four got ready to come home.

One night in an air raid the drawer boy was outside. The tall English girls and his friend were together and safe in the butler's pantry of a large and empty house. They lit candles and made jokes about where the other one might be. Well, he was down the street, looking at another large house. Probably staring at the wrought iron, or memorizing the slope of the roof. The front door of the house flew off when the shell hit, and the drawer boy watched it come for him.

A doctor took two inches of copper plate out of the boy's head, from the front door knocker. The doctor put in 26 millimetres of stainless steel. Before the doctor could close up the wound, the boy's memory escaped.

His hair grew back and the boy's three friends slowly put his memory back, too. One day he woke up and remembered right and left, and up and down. One day he woke up and remembered he loved the taller English girl. They got ready to go home again, talked about their plans again. They showed the drawer boy pictures he made of the house all four would live in, pictures he had made before the front door came: he could not remember making the pictures, but he agreed to the plan. They would come home. There would be a double wedding. There was money enough for one piece of land. The house would be built on a farm they would share, and it would be two houses joined. Two families would be started, life would begin for the four friends.

They came home. There was a double wedding, the drawer boy recited a poem from the stolen book. They bought one piece of land. They started to build the house. They bought a car. They bought an old black car.

ANGUS   Right.

MORGAN   The taller English girl loved to drive, and one day she and the tall English girl went in the old black car to a berry bush the farmer boy had shown them. Coming home there were two pails of raspberries between them on the seats. They knew what side of the road to be on. They did. An old army transport came over the hill on their side, coming toward them; the transport was passing a horse. The taller English girl turned, turned her side of the old black car into the transport because she knew they could not miss. Her side of the old car was just ruined. Not a scratch on the tall girl's side. But the tall girl died, too.

ANGUS   Right. My Sally. My… Sally. Your?

MORGAN   My Frances. Then the two tall English girls went to a hill, both in the same carriage, pulled by a horse. The hill is the highest point in the county. That's where they are now. And then it was the two friends again. And the drawer makes bread and adds rows of numbers in his head, and the farmer farms and tends to the place on the hill.

ANGUS   Right. Morgan. I smell bread.

MORGAN   You do? How do you feel? How's your head?

ANGUS   No. I smell bread.

MORGAN   *(jumping up)* Jesus.

> *MORGAN runs into the kitchen to rescue the bread. MILES escapes without being seen.*
>
> *(pulls the burnt bread out of the oven)* Jesus! Angus! Goddam it!

ANGUS   Nineteen thousand, four hundred and forty... five.

Act One, Scene Six

> *Late that night. MILES comes into the kitchen. He pulls out his notebook.*

MILES   Two friends built a cabin with nails they stole from.... Two friends grew up together; one was a farmer, one drew pictures. They made plans, they went to school. They went off to war. They shot their guns in the air and sang war songs. They had three boots between them. They met two English girls, one tall and one taller.

> *ANGUS enters in his pajamas. He's searching for something. As MILES watches, he goes carefully through the kitchen, beginning again with the blank space on the wall. Eventually, he sees MILES.*

ANGUS   Hey! Who are you??

MILES   My name's Miles. I'm staying with you and Morgan to learn about farming so I can write a play about it.

ANGUS   Okay. Hello, Miles.

> *ANGUS sits down at the table.*

MILES   Did you come down for something? It's a couple of hours until we have to rotate the crops.

ANGUS   Eh?

MILES	Were you looking for something?
ANGUS	Sure.
MILES	What?
ANGUS	No idea.
MILES	…Should you go to bed then?
ANGUS	You bet.

ANGUS gets up, hesitates, then heads outside. MILES follows, and watches as ANGUS stands, looking at the stars.

MILES	Angus?
ANGUS	You bet.
MILES	Nice night.
ANGUS	That's right.

A pause.

You organize it into sections. The whole sky. It's just pieces. No bigger than you. Then you count it.

A pause.

See?

MILES	Uh huh.

ANGUS goes inside. He repeats exactly the moves from earlier, looking for something. MILES watches him for a while.

Can I help you find it?

ANGUS	Jeez. I couldn't tell ya. You hungry?
MILES	Not really.
ANGUS	Me neither.

ANGUS leaves. After a moment, MILES returns to the notebook.

Act One, Scene Seven

An afternoon a couple of days later. MORGAN and ANGUS enter.

ANGUS   …That was exactly right, wasn't it? The tractor? Them two girls were the tires and the one fella on the other's shoulders and he was driving the fella and the two girls, because *they were the tractor*. And telling about the tractor breaking down when the harvest hasta come in, and how you gotta be awake when you go over hills and the like: the fella sitting on top of the fella's shoulders, talking away to us while he's driving the tractor. That was exactly right.

MORGAN   Uh huh.

ANGUS   And that girl who came out and said she was… was…

MORGAN   Alison Lobb.

ANGUS   That's right. D'you know for a long while there I thought she *was* Alison Lobb? I thought good lord, Alison Lobb's lost her senses and gone up there on the stage and was talking to us. It wasn't, you know. That was an actress. Acting.

MORGAN   I know.

ANGUS   I *laughed*. And then… Miles comes out and starts with that story about the two tall English girls and the war and all, in that funny voice, and all of a sudden I realized—it's you! He's pretending to be you and that's why I knew the story just before he said each word. He told it just the way you do! I remembered all of it as he said it, I could have said it along with him…. Hey! Shit! That other fella! The simple-looking fella he was telling the story to! That was me! The one fella was you and the other one was supposed to be me! Jesus, that was something. That was us.

MORGAN   That was us.

ANGUS   He got us, didn't he? Miles. He got us.

MORGAN   He did.

ANGUS   He did. I'll never forget that. I can't wait until everyone—

MORGAN	Angus? Want a sandwich?
ANGUS	Sure.

> *ANGUS gets sandwich materials out of fridge, starts to make a couple.*

	I'll tell yuh, Morgan, that was just, I never seen…
MORGAN	Angus? How many stars you count last night?
ANGUS	618 I never counted before. 1079 I already did.
MORGAN	Got a new total?
ANGUS	Sure. 22,757. New total.
MORGAN	Good. What did we do today?
ANGUS	Aaww. We just got back.
MORGAN	From where.
ANGUS	From… town?
MORGAN	What on earth were we doing in town?
ANGUS	Well, Morgan, I don't know. We were… I don't… I'm hungry, though. Sandwich?
MORGAN	Okay.

> *MORGAN sees MILES coming into the yard. Goes out to intercept him.*

MILES	What'd you think of the rehearsal? A lot of it's pretty rough, but I thought some of it went…
MORGAN	You get out of here.
MILES	…I'm sorry?
MORGAN	You heard. Get out. You can't stay here.
MILES	Morgan, hold it. You're upset I used that story and didn't tell you—I wanted that to be a surprise.
MORGAN	It was. You put that in your play and I'll see to it you never put it on.
MILES	Look, if I didn't get the story exactly right, it's because I only heard it once. You can give me the details, we can

work on it together. It's important. We're here to get your history and give it back to you.

MORGAN It ain't.... You can't use that. It's private between Angus and me and I don't want people to hear it.

MILES Everyone around here must know the story already. I just want to tell it to them in the play, so they can see how important it is.

MORGAN Just get out of here. You can't stay. You lied.

MILES What does Angus say about it?

MORGAN Angus' already forgotten it, thank God. You oughta be ashamed, coming here, stealing...

MILES Morgan, listen to me. It's the only thing I got in the show right now. If I cut this scene, which the director loves, by the way, I'm out of the show. Produce or die, remember?

ANGUS comes outside, sees MILES.

ANGUS Hey!!!

MILES Hello, Angus. My name's—

ANGUS Miles! We saw you! You were Morgan and that other fella was me! You got us!

MILES ...That's right. You remember the play?

MORGAN You know who that is?

ANGUS Sure. You're Miles, and you're staying with Morgan and me while you learn about farming and write that play! You were Morgan. You told about us. God! I'll never forget it. Come in and have a sandwich, Miles.

MILES *(to MORGAN)* Has he ever...?

MORGAN Never recognized anyone but me.

ANGUS You *were* him. You sounded just like Morgan. Come in and have a sandwich.

MORGAN He has to go now. He's gonna get his things and leave.

ANGUS Why?

MILES I don't know, exactly.

ANGUS   Well, that's just silly. You can't go. Just got here.

MORGAN   He's leaving.

ANGUS   Why?

MILES   Because of what I did on stage.

ANGUS   Whatareyuh…?

MILES   Your story. About the two tall English girls. Morgan says I can't use it.

ANGUS   Oh. Well. Shit. That's not a story. That's us. You have to use that.

> *MILES and MORGAN stare at each other. ANGUS goes back inside.*

He has to use that. He's here because he's…. Miles! Get in here! Kinda sandwich you want?

> *MILES goes inside and sits with ANGUS. Blackout.*

Act Two, Scene One

*The next day. MILES sits on the ground outdoors.
There are two piles of gravel beside him: a big pile and
a little pile. He takes a stone from the big pile, dunks it in
a bucket of soapy water, scrubs it with a vegetable brush,
and dries it carefully with a small towel. Then he puts it
onto the small pile.*

ANGUS sits on the back step, listening.

MILES   …and I have these two friends. From university. They're funny. They talk alike and they sort of dress alike and they're always together. And because I'm sad, my stepfather calls them up and says "he mopes around wearing black all day, come and visit and cheer him up," and so they do. Except what my stepfather really wants them to do is spy on me, in case I get it into my head that I want to kill him.

ANGUS   Why would you…?

MILES   Because like I said, he killed my father and married my mum and my father told me to. Sort of. His ghost sort of told me to.

ANGUS   Right.

MILES   Their names are Rosencrantz and Guildenstern.

ANGUS   You're kidding.

MILES   I am not.

ANGUS   Hee hee.

MILES   So they show up and I know right off that they're here to spy on me for my stepfather. So I put on an antic disposition. I pretend to go mad—I threaten them and call them names and kick them out. Except you start to wonder: am I acting mad, or am I really going mad? I'm all sad and angry, I keep hearing voices, and I can't decide what to do so I do nothing and that makes me even worse.

	I start treating my girlfriend really badly, I yell at her and call her bad names, I just treat her terribly until she goes mad for sure and drowns herself in a pond.
ANGUS	Miles. You went mad.
MILES	And then I yell at my mother. And—Angus, you aren't baking, are you?
ANGUS	Who knows. You yelled at your mum?
MILES	And then I kill this nice old guy who talked all the time. I stabbed him through the arras.
ANGUS	The arras. Ouch. Were you mad then? Or just pretending?
MILES	Well, you still weren't sure. You still couldn't tell.
ANGUS	But, could you?
MILES	I… yes. I think I was a little mad then. I think stabbing a guy makes you go even more mad.
ANGUS	Oh, I know.
MILES	Anyway, by the time I finish talking to my mum and stabbing the old guy, I decide I have to kill my stepfather.
ANGUS	Cause of hearing your dad's voice?
MILES	Yes.
ANGUS	But, Miles! What if the voice in your head is just some voice? You can't go killing people because of that.
MILES	That's right…
ANGUS	I mean, Jesus, what if everybody acted that way?
MILES	I know.
ANGUS	Killing people just 'cause of something they heard in their head once or twice.
MILES	I know.
ANGUS	Everybody did that, there'd be no one left. S'not right.
MILES	You're right. That's what I'm so worried about. That's why I went mad.

MORGAN comes in from the barn. As he passes MILES:

MORGAN   Hurry up. I'll need that gravel by after lunch.

ANGUS   Morgan! Hello.

MORGAN goes inside.

ANGUS   That's a tough job you've got.

MILES   Yeah, the actor's life's a difficult one.

ANGUS   No. The…

Points at what MILES is doing.

MILES   Have you ever done this?

ANGUS   Well, I guess I must of, sometime. Tough job. So, what… where…. Oh! Your stepfather. Didja kill him?

MILES   Well, not right away. My girlfriend's brother comes home, he's mad at me because she killed herself, so we have a couple of sword fights, everybody takes some drugs sort of by accident, and then everybody dies.

ANGUS   Everybody dies by accident?

MILES   Sort of.

ANGUS   Helluvan accident.

MILES   And then I die too.

ANGUS   I should hope so. Did people clap?

MILES   Oh, yeah. People loved it. The people that saw it. The critics hated it.

ANGUS   Why?

MILES   I don't know. They said I was too Canadian.

ANGUS   Well, that makes sense.

MORGAN comes back outside. He has a dessert fork.

Morgan. Hello. He went mad.

MORGAN   *(to MILES)* Here. Know what this is? This is a short handled insilage fork. After the gravel's washed, I want you to muck out the cow stalls. Using this. Cows have been eating corn lately, and not all of it gets digested. You use this to retrieve the undigested corn and put it into a bucket. We feed the chickens that fortified corn. You understand me?

MILES   Yes.

MORGAN leaves.

He must think I'm so stupid.

ANGUS   Oh, he does.

MILES   As if I'd go through all the cow crap with this. With a stupid little fork.

ANGUS   It's crazy.

MILES   It sure is.

ANGUS   I'll get you a spoon. Tell me another.

MILES   Let's see. Did one about a family from out around here called the Donnellys. Bad bunch. They were so nasty to so many people that one night a mob came and burned down their house.

ANGUS   Jeez. Who made that up? That Shakespeare?

MILES   No, a Canadian wrote it, but it's not made up. It's a true story. It really happened.

ANGUS   Whadda ya mean! It was on stage, wasn't it? It was a play.

MILES   It was a play from a true story. Like the one that we're making up now. It's a play about farmers, but the stories we tell in it are true ones. Like the story I heard Morgan tell you.

ANGUS   The two tall English girls.

MILES   Right.

ANGUS   Tell it.

MILES   I don't think so, Angus.

ANGUS   Go on.

MILES   No, I don't think Morgan would like it.

ANGUS   Course he would. Why wouldn't he?

MILES	Well, because it's his story. His and yours. And he should tell it to you, not me.
ANGUS	Okay.
MILES	Sorry.
ANGUS	No.

A pause.

What if you pretended you were him. You be Morgan and I'll pretend I'm Angus and you tell it that way.

MILES	I can't do that.
ANGUS	Can too.
MILES	No, I can't.
ANGUS	Sure, just pretend you're Morgan sitting there washing rocks and you think to yourself, "Geez, I'd better tell Angus that there tall girl story before I do another thing," and then say "Angus" and I'll say "What?" and you say the story of the two English tall girls now hurry up.
MILES	No, look, I can't. It's Morgan's story to tell. It's not right that I start telling it to you.
ANGUS	Oh. Unless you're up on stage telling everybody, right?
MILES	Uhh. Right.
ANGUS	Oh.
MILES	Right, so…
ANGUS	It'd be okay for me though? To tell it?
MILES	Of course. Yes. I'd love to hear it.
ANGUS	Okay. I'll pretend to be you pretending to be Morgan telling the story.

Now, would I be on a stage, or…

MILES	No. You're just sitting on the back step.
ANGUS	Oh. Right. Okay then.

ANGUS contorts himself and raises his voice an octave.

Now I'm you.

He hunches over and drops his voice two octaves.

And now I'm you being Morgan. Any good?

MILES	Perfect.
ANGUS	Perfect. How's it start?
MILES	*(He pulls out his notebook.)* Once there were two friends…
ANGUS	Once there were two friends.

As MILES leads ANGUS through the story, MILES falls into his MORGAN persona until there are two slightly grotesque MORGANs telling the story back and forth.

MILES	Two boys. They played hockey together, they did everything together.
ANGUS	Boys who played hockey. And everything.
MILES	The one boy drew pictures.
ANGUS	The one boy drew pictures. The drawer boy.
MILES	Yes. He drew pictures of a cabin. Inside and out, lots of pictures. Then they built the cabin.
ANGUS	Drawer boy drew a cabin inside and out. Then they stole nails and played hookey and built the cabin.
MILES	And then they went off to war together.
ANGUS	And then they went off to war together.
MILES	They fought together and yelled together and sang when it was loudest. They had three boots between them.
ANGUS	They fired up in the air together and hid and sang together when it got too loud and… three boots.
MILES	In England they met two girls…
ANGUS	One tall and one taller.
MILES	The taller one liked the drawer.
ANGUS	And the tall one liked Morgan. Liked me.

MILES	The tall girl and the farmer would talk all night; the taller girl and the drawer would walk all night and talk. One girl would talk to the other boy about the boy she liked, so would the other girl to the other boy.
ANGUS	…They talked.
MILES	When they were done talking their plans were as complete as something the boy would draw.
ANGUS	When they were done talking, they had a picture of the next thing they would make together, the four of them. They came home and had a double wedding…
MILES	No, Angus. Next is the air raid. The front door flying. Remember?
ANGUS	Uh huh. But. I don't want to.
MILES	Okay.
ANGUS	They went home. There was a double wedding; he said the stolen poem; they started the house, the two houses joined.
MILES	Right.
ANGUS	Where?
MILES	Where what.
ANGUS	Where's the houses joined and separate?
MILES	I don't know.
ANGUS	He said, you said: "They started to build the house."
MILES	You're right.
ANGUS	Where?
MILES	Let's ask him later.
ANGUS	Okay.
MILES	They bought a car.
ANGUS	They bought a black car. Now, Angus, you say "my Sally."
MILES	My Sally. Your…?
ANGUS	My Frances. Your Sally loved to drive the car, the black car. To where raspberries grew wild.

	A horse came the other way, and the army headed straight for my Frances but my Sally, your Sally… Sally…
MILES	She turned her side into the truck, to save her friend, Angus. Your Sally tried to save Frances.
ANGUS	She… yes.
MILES	And now it's the two friends again.
ANGUS	And now it's the…. No. They got taken in a cart to the highest point in the county. Buried there.
MILES	Yes. That's right. And now it's the two friends again.
ANGUS	And now it's…

I've never been there. The highest point in the county. Hey.

> *He's being led by a memory so faint he behaves as though he's smelling something. ANGUS walks inside. He drops to his knees, and pulls up a floorboard. He pulls out a beat-up metal tube, khaki green, about three feet long. He opens the tube and pulls out several architectural drawings. He spreads them out on the table.*

The houses joined. Together and separate.

> *MORGAN enters. ANGUS greets him without looking up.*

Morgan! Hello! The houses joined. They never got started. Did they? You said they did. I want to go to them.

MORGAN	*(to MILES)* How did you find these?
MILES	I didn't.
MORGAN	How did you find these.
ANGUS	You hid them. I saw you. You didn't see me.
MORGAN	You remember that?
ANGUS	I… I guess I do…
MILES	You made these?
ANGUS	The two houses joined up. I drew these. Separate and joined. I was the drawer boy.

MORGAN	You did. You were. *end*
ANGUS	I am. I want to see her, Morgan. Take me to where they are. Up on that hill. The tallest point. *(to MILES)* You should come, too. You did this. Let's go right now.
	ANGUS goes outside.
MORGAN	No, Angus. You're baking.
ANGUS	Well, just—turn off the damn… whatever that is! I want to go now. My Sally.
MORGAN	*(following ANGUS out)* Listen to me. We can't go, Angus. Now just stop this.
ANGUS	Can too. I have to.
MORGAN	Angus! Make me a sandwich. I'm hungry.
ANGUS	Make you…? Make your own damn sandwich, old fella! I got to…
	Damn it. I WANT TO GO.
	MILES comes outside.
	I been waiting so long. I never, why'd you not ever take me? That's my Sally. That's my WIFE.
MILES	Angus. I'm sure he must have. You don't remember things, you know.
ANGUS	I want to go to them. I'll remember them now.
MORGAN	I'm hungry. I want to eat something.
ANGUS	I'll cook once we get back. Let's go. Why'd you never take me there before?
MORGAN	No.
ANGUS	Yes.
MORGAN	No.
ANGUS & MILES	Yes!
MORGAN	*(to MILES)* I beg your pardon?
MILES	Well, I mean, he seems to want to go. I just thought—

MORGAN	Would you excuse us, please? Wait inside.
MILES	Sure.
ANGUS	He'll come too!
MILES	Yes, but, I'm just going to go inside for a while.

He does.

ANGUS	I'll get the truck, or, you should get the truck, you know where we're going. Plus, do I know how to drive?
MORGAN	Angus, I'm tired. I want my lunch. There's so much I need to do this afternoon.
ANGUS	Not more important than this! There's a picture of the place in my head, the tallest spot, I want to go and match it. Now.
MORGAN	Feed came this morning. Usual amount, and I wrote Wally a cheque. Can we cover it?
ANGUS	Leaves forty-four dollars and sixteen cents. Dairy give us ninety-one twenty-one in the next three days, we can cover the loan and have sixteen-oh-eight to spare *now let's go.*
MORGAN	Angus. No. We aren't going.

A pause.

ANGUS	You eat lunch first. *Then.*
MORGAN	No. Not then.
ANGUS	Yes then. Go now and quick, there's some, there's some… something for a sandwich in the… thing, quick. Go. I'll wait out here.
MORGAN	Listen to me.
ANGUS	You go! I'll wait patiently for you to come out and we'll go see—
MORGAN	Listen.
ANGUS	—SEE MY SALLY.

ANGUS holds his head, has to sit.

MORGAN	Angus, are you—

ANGUS	GO IN! *Go in and come out.*
	MORGAN goes inside. He starts to make a sandwich.
MILES	I believe he will remember this time, if you take him.
MORGAN	I'm not taking him.
ANGUS	Morgan. Done yet?
MILES	But why?
ANGUS	Morgan.
MORGAN	That's between him and me.
MILES	Fine, I don't want to interfere—
ANGUS	Morgan! Time's up!
MILES	—But he's better now, he seems better. Since rehearsal. He's remembering things. And he wants to go.
MORGAN	I told him no, and I'm telling you no.
ANGUS	*(holding his head)* Aw, God.
	Moorgan!
	Silence while MORGAN finishes making the sandwich, sits, and begins to eat.
	Morgan! Let's go!
	Morgan!
	Mooorgan! You got to drive!
	Moooorgan!!
	ANGUS is in more and more pain.
MILES	Morgan, Jesus…
MORGAN	How's the gravel coming?
MILES	I'll take him myself. Just tell me where it is.
ANGUS	Mooorgan! Get the… truck!
MORGAN	You got too much to do. Gravel and then the muckin' out.
ANGUS	Aaaaahhh.

Morgan! Morgan.

MILES   This is just cruel.

ANGUS   (*suddenly not in pain*) Morgan! Get the Jeep!

MILES   Morgan, for God's sake.

ANGUS   Get a, we need a Jeep! Don't tell anyone! Morgan!

MORGAN   (*goes to the door*) Angus! Come indoors.

ANGUS   Morgan! Hello. We need a ride. We can't tell anyone. We got to go.

MORGAN   Come inside.

> *They go inside.*

ANGUS   What did you do to get us passes? Sergeant says don't tell anyone and be back by oh six hundred. Jesus Morgan! Miles. You can't come.

MORGAN   Angus, listen—

ANGUS   Sally will just—let's go now. Surprise them.

MORGAN   Angus? You need to go upstairs. To bed, now.

ANGUS   To hell with that! They're waiting for us. Did you call? Did you?

MORGAN   I…. Yes. I did.

ANGUS   I knew it! Jesus, you did. Goddam it! You set it all up.

MORGAN   That's right. I did.

ANGUS   Ha ha, yuh bastard! Let's go. Miles. You can't go. The girls are waiting, but we got just the two passes. Morgan set it up.

MILES   Angus. I'm sorry. I don't understand you.

MORGAN   This happened.

MILES   What?

MORGAN   I got leave for the two of us overnight. It was his birthday. It was a surprise.

MILES   Angus, you remember?

MORGAN   This is your fault.

ANGUS   You've got to lend me some shoes, mine are still wet from the ditch. Sergeant says we have to… we have to be back…

> *His headache resumes.*

Morgan? It's too bright.

MORGAN   Let's go, Angus. Upstairs.

ANGUS   No! She's waiting with… to give me… cufflinks.

MORGAN   You can't go like that. Can you.

ANGUS   No. Not like this.

MORGAN   Let's go up and get your uniform on.

ANGUS   Okay.

MORGAN   Get you that shoe.

ANGUS   Let's… hurry. *(looks at MILES)* Hey. Who're you?

MORGAN   That's the man who did this to you.

> *MORGAN leads ANGUS upstairs.*

Act Two, Scene Two

> *Late that night. ANGUS walks into the kitchen. As in the first act, he's looking for something. He comes across the architectural drawings.*

ANGUS   God with honour hang your head,
Groom, and grace you, bride, your bed,
With lissome scions, sweet scions,
Out of hallowed bodies bred.

Each be other's comfort kind:
Deep, deeper than divined,—

> *He looks up.*

Morgan?

He gets no response. He goes back to the blueprints.

I want to…

He looks out the door; he looks back toward the stairs.

I'll go. I'll go now.

And he does. Out the back door and off into the night. After a moment, MORGAN comes into the kitchen.

MORGAN   Angus?

He sees the open back door and goes out.

Angus? Angus!!

He walks off. MILES come into the kitchen.

MILES   What is it?

MORGAN comes back into the house. He pulls on his boots, puts on a jacket.

MORGAN   He's gone.

MILES   Oh, no. He went to the graveyard. I'll go…

MORGAN   You stay here.

MILES   Look: I'm "the man who did this." I want to help.

MORGAN   *You stay here.*

MORGAN leaves.

Act Two, Scene Three

Dawn. MILES sits in the kitchen. He waits impatiently. He gets up, goes outside. He sees the two piles of rocks left over from the day before. He picks up a rock, dunks it in the pail of water, dries it with the cloth, and sets it on the small pile. He does this again, distractedly. Then he looks around surreptitiously, picks up the bucket of water, dumps the water on the larger pile of rocks, pats the pile

> *dry a couple of times and then pushes the big pile and the little pile together. MORGAN enters.*

MILES   Any luck?

MORGAN   No.

> *MORGAN goes inside. He doesn't know what to do with himself. He makes a sandwich. MILES goes in. ANGUS, his arm bleeding, walks through the yard, and then off.*

MILES   He'll turn up.

> *Pause.*

Finished the gravel.

MORGAN   Huh? Oh. Goes in the culvert.

MILES   Sure. Is the culvert that shed thing out behind the barn?

MORGAN   No, it's… never mind. I'll do it.

> *A pause.*

MILES   What about the graveyard?

MORGAN   What about it.

MILES   Did you look there?

MORGAN   No.

MILES   But that's where he wanted to go.

MORGAN   I'm gonna say this once, as nice as I can under the circumstances: You are not being helpful.

MILES   Fine. I'm sorry. Tell me how I can help.

MORGAN   Go to the henhouse. Shuffle the eggs.

MILES   Morgan…

MORGAN   Take the eggs out from underneath each chicken, put them under a different chicken.

MILES   Look.

MORGAN   That way, they don't raise a fuss when we take their eggs away for good.

MILES   Stop it.

MORGAN   And no chicken has to suffer.

MILES   Tell me why you wouldn't take him to the graveyard. Why you won't look for him there now.

MORGAN   Why? Your play not long enough yet?

MILES   Because I did something to Angus and I hurt you and I don't know how I did that. And I want to fix it.

MORGAN   I'll fix it.

MILES   Tremendous. Fix it. Go to the graveyard and get him. Go now.

MORGAN   Cows need to be milked.

MILES   I'll milk the goddamn cows!

MORGAN   Oh, you will, will you? Think you could figure out the milking machine on your own?

MILES   Yes. I do.

          ANGUS walks into the yard.

MORGAN   You can't recognize the useful end of a shovel. You go out there, the barn'll fall over.

MILES   I'll do it. Go. Or I'll call the cops and send them up there for him.

MORGAN   You'll what?

MILES   And, I'll tell them that you knew he was out wandering around, and you wouldn't go to get him.

MORGAN   You're gonna call the police?

MILES   I…. No, of course not. I just, I don't understand it. We both know where he is, we both know why he went there, and I can't figure out why you won't—

MORGAN   Stop trying.

MILES   —Why you won't go and get him. He could be hurt, he could be, God knows what. Jesus, Morgan. Don't you care?

MORGAN   You watch your step, young man.

MILES   Tell me why you won't go. Tell me why you're just standing there.

MORGAN   *(tosses his truck keys to MILES)* You go.

MILES   Okay. Thank you. I will.

> *MILES turns to go. Before he gets outside, he stops suddenly. He turns to MORGAN.*

It's not true. What you tell him isn't true.

That's why you won't go. Isn't it.

MORGAN   You get out of here.

> *MILES leaves; he sees ANGUS.*

MILES   Morgan!

ANGUS   *(to MILES)* What did you…?

> *MORGAN comes outdoors.*

MORGAN   Angus! Are you alright? What happened to you? Where did you get to?

ANGUS   *(to MORGAN)* What did he mean?

MORGAN   *(to MILES)* You leave us alone?

MILES   Sure.

> *He goes.*

MORGAN   Angus? You alright? Come inside.

> *ANGUS goes in.*

Sit down. Lemme look at that arm. How did this happen?

ANGUS   "It's not true. What you tell him." I heard.

MORGAN   You hungry? Want a sandwich?

ANGUS   No, I heard, I… what did he mean—

MORGAN   Jesus, Angus. You haven't walked off for some time. Once I found you up in the mow, looked all day, and your one leg had gone through a hole and you were just stuck there. You didn't care. Looking off, like you were waiting for a train or something. Do you know, I pulled you out, carried you down and it took you till the next day to come back to yourself. You scared me. What were you thinking about? You'd do it when we were kids, I'd find you up a tree somewhere, you'd be staring off, I'd be yelling "Angus, Angus," and you'd come back to yourself, climb back down, ask what day it was. It was funny when we were kids.

I'm gonna make you something to eat and I want you to eat it.

ANGUS   No, please. Listen to me.

            MORGAN goes to the sink, gets a spoonful of water, and gives it to ANGUS.

            Okay, but. Please, tell me what—

MORGAN   No. Hush now.

            MORGAN begins sandwichmaking. ANGUS looks down at the blueprints.

ANGUS   The houses joined. Together and separate.

            A pause.

            I drew these.

MORGAN   Yes.

ANGUS   Don't remember doing that. Remember him hiding them, though. I saw him hide them.

MORGAN   Saw who?

ANGUS   Him. He didn't see me.

MORGAN   Angus. Look at me. Who am I?

ANGUS   You're the man who did this to me.

MORGAN   What's my name.

ANGUS   Don't you know?

MORGAN   Look at me.

ANGUS   You played the farmer boy. You got us.

MORGAN   No, Angus.

ANGUS   Sure.

MORGAN   No, Angus. Please. Tell me who I am.

ANGUS   Why should I?

MORGAN   I want to know if you're okay.

ANGUS   I don't care.

I was in the dark, walking, and I got stopped. I heard a voice. It was a ghost, it stopped me, it warned me against you.

MORGAN   What?

ANGUS   It told me what you did. It told me I should be afraid of you. It said: HE KILLED YOUR FATHER. HE MARRIED YOUR MUM.

MORGAN   Angus, you're scaring me.

ANGUS   *(He finally looks at MORGAN.)* Good. Okay. Listen to me.

I was just pretending. I was pretending I was mad. There was no voice. It was my antic disposition. Morgan. I'm scared.

Listen, I was out there, and I heard. He said, Miles said "It's not true. What you tell him isn't true." I heard.

MORGAN   You did.

ANGUS   Yes. Miles said "It's not true. What you tell him isn't true." Did he mean me?

MORGAN   Yes.

ANGUS   Oh. What did he mean?

MORGAN   He means I lied. I lied to you.

ANGUS   Is that true?

MORGAN   Yes.

ANGUS   Oh. Okay.

You lied. You're a bastard.

God. Look. The houses joined.

Where's Miles. I want him to tell it.

MORGAN   Not now.

ANGUS   Yes, now. I want Miles to. He, what did he do?

Oh, God, Morgan.

MORGAN   What's wrong?

ANGUS   What'd he do to me? I have, in my head…

MORGAN   What. Tell me.

ANGUS   Just everything. Just… everything. It came all night. Listen:

I'm a boy and I have a cough and a nosebleed on my shirt. On my short pants. I remembered that. Then, another time, I'm writing a test and the smell of you sittin' beside me, smell of you failing it. I remember France, that boy running away. You would not shoot the boy running away. Sally, the first sight of her from behind in that church. Oh, God, oh no, I remember that. Her hair, my finger trapped in the pages of the hymn book. And then, I got hurt, God, the noise, I'm lying on the ground…

I remember when my head didn't hurt, I think. I remember Miles who was you on that… stage. I remember the double wedding.

MORGAN   You remember the double wedding?

ANGUS   I do. I stood up, I said: God with honour hang your head, groom—

MORGAN   You remember getting hurt?

ANGUS   I do. I remember the door flying. At me.

The three of you safe and me on my way to you and I got stopped by the architecture.

MORGAN   No, that's, oh, Jesus.

ANGUS   I remember everything.

MORGAN   No you don't.

ANGUS   Yes. Yes I do! It came all night. I walked. I was looking for them.

MORGAN   You remember the story. What he said on stage.

ANGUS   No. I remember *it*.

MORGAN   What was in your hand?

ANGUS   My hand?

MORGAN   What were you carrying?

ANGUS   Nothing. I don't think...

MORGAN   What you just told me is what I've told you all these years. That's our story. What you had in your hand was a bottle of cheap brandy, given to me in a card game. I sent you to fetch it. Remember? *We laughed*, and I made you get it. You were safe, and I sent you out, you understand? Angus? I did that. I did that to you. That's the first thing.

ANGUS   That's the first thing? See. you're a bastard.

              What do I remember?

MORGAN   You remember the story.

ANGUS   Aw, God.

MORGAN   Angus. What'd I get for that car.

ANGUS   Car?

MORGAN   The black car.

ANGUS   It got wrecked. The army truck.

MORGAN   Did it? If you can remember, then remember.

ANGUS   Don't.

MORGAN   What'd I get for that car.

ANGUS   It got wrecked, my Sally was driving and she turned it into the truck—

MORGAN   No. It's a number.

ANGUS   I don't want to. I want him—I want the story.

MORGAN   *How much'd I get for that car?*

ANGUS   Hundred and ten dollars.

MORGAN   That's right.

ANGUS	Hundred and ten dollars. Oh. From Doug Hamm. It didn't crash.
MORGAN	That's right. We sold it. You do remember.
ANGUS	No I don't.
MORGAN	Angus, listen…
ANGUS	No. It's not true. What you tell him isn't true. I heard.
MORGAN	It is true.
ANGUS	Where's Miles? Hey! Miles! Get in here!
MORGAN	No, Angus, wait.
ANGUS	I want him. Miles!

       MILES runs on.

       (to MILES) You said: "What you tell him isn't true." He said: "I lied." He lied. He's a bastard. Now he says something… else. You have to tell it.

MILES	Morgan'll tell you.
ANGUS	No, he won't. He's a bastard. You will. You know.
MILES	Angus. Do you know what I am? I'm an actor. I play at things. I was playing Morgan when you saw me. But he's here. He's right there, and he can tell you.
ANGUS	He lied. I remember you.
MILES	Listen to me. Do you know what I did just now? I was out in the barn, pretending to be a farmer. All those cows were in agony, they were all begging to be milked and do you know what I did? I hooked the milking machine up to Daisy and switched it on and she groaned and then the whole thing stopped. I broke it. I don't know what I'm doing, Angus. Let Morgan tell you.
ANGUS	You broke the milking machine?
MILES	Yes.
ANGUS	Aw, Jesus.
MORGAN	*(simultaneous with the above)* Aw, Jesus.

MILES	Sorry. You were right. But you don't need to rush out there. Daisy's okay. They're all okay. I milked them by hand.
MORGAN	You milked nine cows by hand?
MILES	Well, a little bit each. Just to take the pressure off. I was standing there amid all these weeping cows. I had to do something. I just sat down, grabbed hold, and got the hang of it pretty fast. I just went from cow to cow, one after another; grab, milk, grab, milk, grab, milk, grab, milk… suddenly, I looked up and it was done.
MORGAN	What'd you do when the bucket got full?
MILES	You're supposed to use a bucket?
ANGUS	Aw, Jesus!
MILES	Okay? I've caused enough trouble. I've got to go. I've got rehearsal…
ANGUS	No! Tell it.
MORGAN	I am. I will.
ANGUS	No. Him.
MILES	Angus, no.
ANGUS	Okay. Both of you. Tell it.
MORGAN	I will, but not with him here.
ANGUS	Yes, with him here. I'm scared. You're scaring me, yuh bastard.
	From the start. Both of you.
MORGAN	Angus, don't—
ANGUS	BOTH OF YOU. Please. So I can match them. Find me in them. I'm starved to know.
MORGAN	Alright.
ANGUS	Right. Go. You start.
MILES	Okay.
ANGUS	But, as him.
MILES	Right.

ANGUS	Like you did, on the… thing.
MILES	I got it.
	(as MORGAN) A couple of boys played shinney and went to school and grew up.
ANGUS	Now you.
MORGAN	They built…
ANGUS	But, as you.
MORGAN	…We built a cabin together. You dreamed it up, I did all the work.
MILES	Stole nails and played hookey and built a cabin. From the drawer boy's pictures.
MORGAN	You were about to go to university. I talked you out of it. The war started, and I talked you into volunteering with me. It was going to be an adventure. We were so excited. No. I was excited, and you were… I talked you into it. We joined up. As soon as we got over there, we were at an airfield, and we saw something. A stupid accident during training. Do you remember?
ANGUS	I…
MORGAN	We watched three men burn to death. We couldn't help. It was awful.
	And then the only thing we did was survive. We never volunteered for anything, we hid when things got bad. We'd use up ammunition by shooting straight up.
MILES	Then, they met two girls.
	One tall, and one taller.
	The taller one liked the drawer, the tall one, the farmer.
MORGAN	They agreed to marry us. They agreed to come home with us. They were friends like we were friends. The four of us were together as much as possible. We would spend whole nights talking, the four of us. You and Sally would take long walks and count the stars. She taught you how. She knew the names of stars, and how to cut the sky up, into

manageable pieces for counting. It was the first thing she gave you.

MILES They made plans. By the time they were done talking, they had a picture of what they would do, like something the one boy would draw.

MORGAN All we had to do was wait out our tour. All we had to do was keep hiding.

Then, one night in an air raid, I sent you out, to get a bottle of brandy I left in Sally's car. We decided we wanted a drink, we were all together, we felt indestructible, because of, because of each other. Like the war was just a dream or something. You took a long time to come back. We made jokes about where you might be. I said to Sally: he's found someone else.

MILES The drawer boy was standing down the street, looking at a large house.

MORGAN You were running like hell down the street, trying to get back. Jesus. You were laughing.

MILES The front door of the house flew off when the shell hit, and the drawer boy watched it come for him.

MORGAN A piece of shrapnel caught you from behind. I watched you get carried through the air. You flew right at me. You nearly died. But you didn't. You woke up. But your memory was… gone.

We came home. They came with us.

There was no double wedding. Sally wanted to wait. Until you were better.

ANGUS But, the stolen poem.

MORGAN You never said it. You've been waiting to say it.

We bought this land. We lived here, in the house that came with the land, English girls in one room, us in the other. The house you designed was never started. We tacked the plans up over there, *(indicates the spot ANGUS looks first when searching)* so that we could see every day what we intended to do. Eventually, they became just a… reminder.

So, one day when you were asleep, when I thought you were asleep, I took them down and I hid them. We did buy an old car, so they could go into town. They were lonely. The car didn't help much.

Sally looked after you. She stayed by you all the time, every minute. She'd watch you wander off, she'd follow behind, hiding behind trees so you wouldn't see. You'd get lost, she'd be there, and she'd bring you back home. She'd clean you. She'd feed you. She gave you medicine from a spoon.

You kept having headaches. They made you different, Angus, they made you mean. Because she was always there, you'd get mean at Sally.

ANGUS At Sally.

MORGAN One day, she was very tired. It was hot, hot like they'd never felt at home. You had another headache. Sally was cooking, baking bread, and you came up to her and without saying a thing you hit her. She cried and cried; she wasn't hurt much, but she was tired. You looked at her, and then you had to ask me who that crying girl was. And it was then that Sally decided to leave.

ANGUS Your Frances…?

MORGAN They were friends. They were here alone.

The day they went, they called a taxi from town. You were asleep. I was here (*in the kitchen doorway*), I couldn't move. The taxi came and I went to help Frances with her suitcase and she said: "This is the worst thing I could do to you. Don't you dare help me do it." She dragged it outside and snarled at the taxi driver when he tried to help her. She was crying from the effort of it. They got in the taxi. They left. I've not heard a word from her in all this time.

When you woke up—

ANGUS No.

MORGAN When you woke up, you knew something was wrong. You went into their room. Looked in the closet, looked under the bed. Tore the room apart. You didn't know what you were looking for. You went through all the rooms, looking, and when you had searched the whole house, you started again. You tore through the house, faster and faster, and you wouldn't stop, Angus, and you couldn't say what you were looking for. Finally, when you were racing up the stairs to start over again, I tackled you. I hauled you down, and we sat on the stairs, and I told you the lie. I told you the story of the black car crashing for the first time. I told it again, and you stopped crying. I told it again, and you fell asleep. I kept telling it cause it made you feel better. Goddam it, it made me feel better.

> *Pause.*

ANGUS I hit my Sally and you lost your…

MORGAN Yes.

ANGUS That's what I did to you. God, you must hate me.

MORGAN I guess I did, Angus.

ANGUS So. That's me. *(to MILES)* He was right. You are the man who did this to me.

MILES I'm late. I should go.

ANGUS Go?

MILES I have to go to work. To rehearse.

ANGUS Yes. You're making a…

MILES That's right.

ANGUS Miles? That was just a story.

MILES I know.

ANGUS No, I mean: you can use it if you want.

MILES Thanks. But. Thanks.

> *MILES takes his notebook out of his pocket and hands it to MORGAN. MILES goes.*

ANGUS That was Miles. He's here staying with you and me while he puts on a play about farming. You told him awful stories.

MORGAN Yes.

> *A pause.*

Well. I'd better go outside and see what he's done to the barn.

> *MORGAN goes. ANGUS follows him into the yard.*

ANGUS   Hey.

> *MORGAN stops, turns.*

You carried me, and all that, around all this time? Since the taxi went?

MORGAN   Yes.

ANGUS   Must be tired. I'll make you a sandwich.

MORGAN   Okay. Thanks.

ANGUS   Uh huh.

> *ANGUS goes inside. He sees the drawings.*

God with honour hang your head,
Groom, and grace you, bride, your bed,
With lissome scions, sweet scions,
Out of hallowed bodies bred.

Each be other's comfort kind:
Deep, deeper than divined,—

MORGAN   *(comes into the yard)* Angus! The bulk cooler's full of milk! He used the milking machine after all. He was, he was lying to us, the silly bugger!

ANGUS   …Divine charity, dear charity,
Fast you ever, fast bind.

Then let the march tread our ears:
I to him turn with tears
Who to wedlock, his wonder wedlock,
Deals triumph and immortal years.

> *As the lights fade, ANGUS takes the drawings and holds them up on the wall where they used to live.*
>
> *The end.*

Michael Healey graduated from the Ryerson Theatre School's acting program in 1985. His first play, a solo show called *Kicked*, premiered at the Fringe of Toronto Festival in 1996. It toured nationally and internationally, and won a Dora Mavor Moore Award for best new play in 1997. He is co-author, with Kate Lynch, of *The Road to Hell*, a pair of one-act comedies which premiered at the Tarragon Theatre in 1999. *The Drawer Boy* premiered at Theatre Passe Muraille in 1999, and won the Dora, Chalmers and Governor General's Awards. It has been produced across North America, in Europe and in Australia, and has so far been translated into Japanese, German and French. *Plan B* premiered at Tarragon Theatre (where he is a playwright-in-residence) in 2001, winning the Dora Award that year. *Rune Arlidge* premiered at Tarragon Theatre in 2004, and was nominated for a Governor General's Award.